Visions of Hope

Visions of Hope

An Illustrated Portrayal of God's Plan for Us

ANNIE HENRIE

DESERET
BOOK

All rights reserved. No part of this book may be reproduced in any form or by any means without permission in writing from the publisher, Deseret Book Company, at permissions@deseretbook.com or P. O. Box 30178, Salt Lake City, Utah 84130. This work is not an official publication of The Church of Jesus Christ of Latter-day Saints. The views expressed herein are the responsibility of the author and do not necessarily represent the position of the Church or of Deseret Book Company.

DESERET BOOK is a registered trademark of Deseret Book Company.

Visit us at DeseretBook.com

Library of Congress Cataloging-in-Publication Data
ISBN: 978-1-60907-819-5

(CIP on file)

Printed in China
R. R. Donnelley, Shenzhen, Guangdong, China

10   9   8   7   6   5   4   3   2   1

Dedicated to the angels in my life, to those who have faithfully

taught me the plan of salvation, and to those who have

supported my art from the very beginning.

Introduction

The idea for an illustrated book of the plan of salvation first surfaced while I was serving as a missionary in southern England. It was a challenging process to help others to see the exquisite beauty of God's plan of happiness for His children, and I wished to be able to help them visualize it. Knowing that the plan of salvation has been crucial in many facets of my life and in the lives of many, many others, I hope to help others realize, reinforce, or rebuild their faith in a greater vision and plan for our existence, the potential we all can achieve, and the deep and abiding love God has for His children.

od's whole purpose—His work and His glory—is to enable each of us to enjoy all his blessings. He has provided a perfect plan to accomplish His purpose. We understood and accepted this plan before we came to the earth. In the scriptures God's plan is called a merciful plan, the plan of happiness, the plan of redemption, and the plan of salvation. —Preach My Gospel, 48

Pre-Earth Life

Life on Earth

BIRTH

DEATH

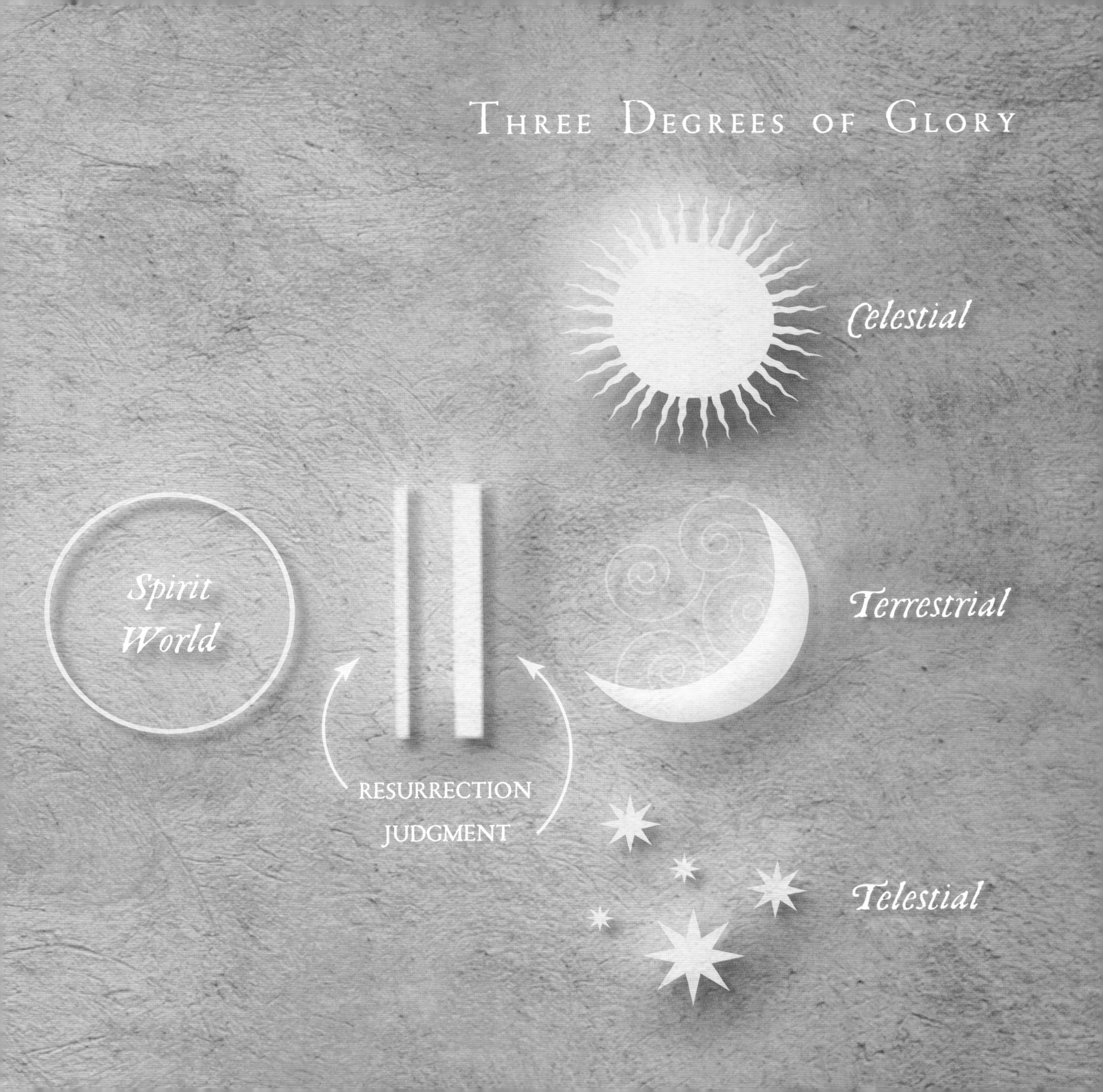

THREE DEGREES OF GLORY

Celestial

Spirit World

Terrestrial

RESURRECTION

JUDGMENT

Telestial

O Lord my God when I in awesome
wonder consider all the worlds thy
hands have made How great thou art

Pre-Earth Life
God's Purpose and Plan for Us

Before I formed thee in the belly

I knew thee;

and before thou camest forth out of the

womb I sanctified thee, and I ordained thee

a prophet unto the nations.

—JEREMIAH 1:5

The Creation

In the beginning was the Word, and the Word
was with God, and the Word was God.
The same was in the beginning with God.

*All things were
made by him;*

and without him was not any thing made that was made.
In him was life; and the life was the light of men.

—John 1:1-4

Agency

Adam fell that men might be . . .

—2 Nephi 2:25

Life on Earth

. . . men are, that they might have

Joy.

FAITH

I would show unto the world that

faith is things
which are hoped for
and not seen;

wherefore, dispute not because ye see not, for ye receive
no witness until after the trial of your faith.

—ETHER 12:6

REPENTANCE

Yea, and as often as my people repent will

I forgive them

their trespasses against me. —MOSIAH 26:30

Therefore, whosoever repenteth, and hardeneth not his

heart, he shall have claim on mercy through mine Only

Begotten Son, unto a remission of his sins; and these

shall enter into my rest.

—ALMA 12:34

Baptism

And the first fruits of repentance is

baptism;

and baptism cometh by faith unto the fulfilling the commandments; and the fulfilling the
commandments bringeth remission of sins.

—Moroni 8:25

GIFT OF THE HOLY GHOST

... And the remission of sins bringeth meekness, and lowliness of heart; and because of meekness and lowliness of heart cometh the visitation of the Holy Ghost, which Comforter filleth with

hope and perfect love,

which love endureth by diligence unto prayer, until the end shall come, when all the saints shall dwell with God.

—Moroni 8:26

Enduring to the End

Wherefore, ye must press forward with a steadfastness in Christ, having a perfect brightness of hope, and a love of God and of all men. Wherefore, if ye shall press forward, feasting upon the word of Christ, and endure to the end, behold, thus saith the Father:

Ye shall have eternal life.

—2 Nephi 31:20

Atonement

And he shall go forth, suffering pains and afflictions and temptations of every kind; and this that the word might be fulfilled which saith he will take upon him the pains and the sicknesses of his people.

And he will take upon him death, that he may loose the bands of death which bind his people; and he will take upon him their infirmities, that his bowels may be

filled with mercy,

according to the flesh, that he may know according to the flesh how to succor his people according to their infirmities.

—Alma 7:11-12

Streams of mercy, never ceasing, call for songs of loudest praise.

Spirit World

. . . the spirits of all men, whether they be good or evil, are taken home to that God who gave them life.

And then shall it come to pass, that the spirits of those who are righteous are received into a state of happiness, which is called paradise,

a state of rest,

a state of peace, where they shall rest from all their troubles and from all care, and sorrow.

—Alma 40:11-12

Resurrection

But there is a resurrection, therefore

the grave hath

no victory,

and the sting of death is swallowed up

in Christ. —Mosiah 16:8

Judgment

IMMORTALITY

Even this mortal shall put on immortality, and this corruption shall put on incorruption, and shall be brought to stand before the bar of God, to be judged of him according to their works whether they be good or whether they be evil. —Mosiah 16:10

Three Degrees of Glory

There are also celestial bodies, and bodies terrestrial:

but the glory of the celestial is one, and the glory of

the terrestrial is another.

There is one glory of the *sun*, and another glory of the

moon, and another glory of the *stars*:

for one star differeth from another star in

glory.

—1 Corinthians 15:40-41

For behold, this is my

work and

my glory—

to bring to pass the immortality and
eternal life of man.

—Moses 1:39

Star of Wonder

Creation

Leaving Eden

Family

Angels Among Us

Balm of Gilead

Baptism

First Blossom

Precious Above All

Streams of Mercy

Between Heaven and Earth

Resurrection Dawn

Glory by Degrees

Together at Last

For more information
about the images in
this book, please visit
AnnieHenrie.com